Winter Morning Walks:

one hundred postcards
to
Jim Harrison

books by Ted Kooser

Ted Kooser

Winter Morning Walks:

**one hundred postcards
to
Jim Harrison**

Carnegie Mellon University Press
Pittsburgh 2000

acknowledgments

The author and publisher are grateful to editors of the following journals in which some of these poems first appeared: *Shenandoah, Midwest Quarterly* and *Tailwind*.

Publication of this book is supported by a grant from the Pennsylvania Council on the Arts.

library of congress control number: 00-135219
ISBN 0-88748-336-4

20 19 18

preface

In the autumn of 1998, during my recovery from surgery and radiation for cancer, I began taking a two-mile walk each morning. I'd been told by my radiation oncologist to stay out of the sun for a year because of skin sensitivity, so I exercised before dawn, hiking the isolated country roads near where I live, sometimes with my wife but most often alone.

During the previous summer, depressed by my illness, preoccupied by the routines of my treatment, and feeling miserably sorry for myself, I'd all but given up on reading and writing. Then, as autumn began to fade and winter came on, my health began to improve. One morning in November, following my walk, I surprised myself by trying my hand at a poem. Soon I was writing every day.

Several years before, my friend Jim Harrison and I had carried on a correspondence in haiku. As a variation on this, I began pasting my morning poems on postcards and sending them to Jim, whose generosity, patience and good humor are here acknowledged. What follows is a selection of one hundred of those postcards.

Ted Kooser
Garland, Nebraska
Spring, 1999

The quarry road tumbles toward me
out of the early morning darkness,
lustrous with frost, an unrolled bolt
of softly glowing fabric, interwoven
with tiny glass beads on silver thread,
the cloth spilled out and then lovingly
smoothed by my father's hand
as he stands behind his wooden counter
(dark as these fields) at Tilden's Store
so many years ago. "Here," he says smiling,
"you can make something special with this."

november

november 9

Rainy and cold.

The sky hangs thin and wet on its clothesline.

A deer of gray vapor steps through the foreground,
under the dripping, lichen-rusted trees.

Halfway across the next field,
the distance (or can that be the future?)
is sealed up in tin like an old barn.

november 10

High winds all night.

Most of the snow passed north of us,
but this morning we're given the fancy white lace
at the edge of that blanket,
every weed on the roadside coated with ice.

Behind the counter at the post office,
somebody's small carton stamped with block letters:
ANGEL MOMENTS WITH SNAIL.

I drive very slowly all the way home.

november 12

4:30 a.m.

On mornings like this, as hours before dawn
I walk the dark hall of the road
with my life creaking under my feet, I sometimes
take hold of the cold porcelain knob
of the moon, and turn it, and step into a room
warm and yellow, and take my seat
at a small wooden table with a border of painted pansies,
and wait for my mother to bring me my bowl.

november 13

Sunny and cold.

Horsetail cirrus miles above,
stretched all the way from Yankton to Wichita.
I stoop on the road, small man in coat and cap,
tying his shoe.

A curled, brown leaf lies on its back,
lifting its undistinguished edges
into the glory of frost.

november 14

In the low forties and clear.

My wife and I walk the cold road
in silence, asking for thirty more years.

There's a pink and blue sunrise
with an accent of red:
a hunter's cap burns like a coal
in the yellow-gray eye of the woods.

november 15

Cold and clear.

An anthem of geese on the wing,
and over the next field
a thin flag of starlings billows and snaps.

At dawn, a sudden fire on a hilltop
four miles east----
Joe Skala's Airstream trailer
reflecting the sun.

november 17

Clouds to the west, clear in the east.

Older this morning, the moon
hid most of her face
behind a round gray mirror.

In a half-hour's walk, I saw
six shooting stars. Celestial notes,
I thought, struck from the high end
of the keyboard.

november 18

Cloudy, dark and windy.

Walking by flashlight
at six in the morning,
my circle of light on the gravel
swinging side to side,
coyote, raccoon, field mouse, sparrow,
each watching from darkness
this man with the moon on a leash.

november 20

Clear and still, a heavy frost.

The pale gray road lit only by stars.
A rabbit runs ahead, then stops
at the edge of the sound of my footsteps,
then runs ahead and stops again,
trembling in darkness
on the cold outer rim of the present.

november 22

Sunny and cool, thin clouds.

In his drab gray overcoat,
unbuttoned and flying out behind,
a stocky, bullet-headed owl
with dirty claws and thick wrists
slowly flaps home
from working the night shift.
He is so tired he has forgotten
his lunchbox, his pay stub.
He will not be able to sleep
in his empty apartment
what with the neighboring blackbirds
flying into his face,
but will stay awake all morning,
round-shouldered and glassy-eyed,
composing a poem about
paradise, perfectly woven
of mouse bones and moist pieces of fur.

november 25

Dark and still.

Shy white calf in the ditch,
round black spot over one eye,
wrong side of the fence
in darkness an hour before light,
I will not tell your master,
Todd Halle,
I found you stiff legged and embarrassed,
head chock full of surprise,
or that his own small moon in eclipse
drifted too close to the road
during the starry November night,
pursuing the sweep
of cool, dewy clouds of black grass.

november 26

Sunny and pleasant.

How is it bittersweet could know
to send its blind gray tendrils
spiralling into the empty limbs
of this particular cedar, dead and bony,
set apart, in winter, on a hillside,
where the bright red berries
in their orange, three-petalled flowers
are shown in such perfection?

november 28

Chilly and clear.

There was a time
when my long gray cashmere topcoat
was cigarette smoke,
and my snappy felt homburg
was alcohol,
and the paisley silk scarf at my neck,
with its fringed end
tossed carelessly over my shoulder,
was laughter rich with irony.
Look at me now.

november 29

Breezy and warm.

A round hay bale,
brown and blind, all shoulders,
huddled, bound tightly
by sky blue nylon twine.
Just so I awoke this morning,
wrapped in fear.

Oh, red plastic flag on a stick
stuck into loose gravel,
driven over, snapped off,
propped up again and again,
give me your courage.

november 30

Sunny and pleasant.

From high above,
the squeak and whimper
of duck's wings.

How hurried they seem,
though the pale blue shell of the sky
stays all day long
and has a pearl to finish.

december

december 1

Sunny and cold.

The long, December shadows
of bare trees
run far away from the woods.

At sunrise, they cross a red pasture
and, though softened and torn
by stones and weeds,
strike out into the trees
on the opposite side,
leaving dark trails through the frost.

december 2

Clear and cool.

Walking in darkness, in awe,
beneath a billion indifferent stars
at quarter to six in the morning,
the moon already down
and gone, but keeping a pale lamp burning
at the edge of the west,
my shoes too loud in the gravel
that, faintly lit, looks to be little more
than a contrail of vapor,
so thin, so insubstantial it could,
on a whim, let me drop through it
and out of the day,
but I have taught myself
to place one foot ahead of the other
in noisy confidence
as if each morning might be trusted,
as if the sounds I make might buoy me up.

december 3

Clear and cool.

I have been sitting here resting
after my morning stroll, and the sun
in its soft yellow work gloves
has come in through the window
and is feeling around on the opposite wall,
looking for me, having seen me
cheerfully walking along the road
just as it rose, having followed me home
to see what I have to be happy about.

december 4

Foggy and dripping.

I was alive and looking
the right direction
when hundreds of starlings
were perched on the sky,
or so it seemed,
though they were really
sprinkled all over
the aluminum roof of a barn
that in fog was sky,
the color and wetness of sky.
They made a noise
like water dripping as they pecked
at the slippery gray,
but only for the instant
in which I was to be their witness,
for then, without a sound,
both sky and roof went blank,
and cleanly separate,
and every bird was gone.

december 7

New snow.

Some hunter, shooting out of season,
maybe last night with a spotlight,
has subtracted a good sized deer
from these woods when nobody else
was around but six inches of snow
to take account of it. There's a track
where he dragged the carcass down
through the trees to a frozen stream
and then over the ice and then up
through the weeds to the county road
where he lifted it into a pickup,
stomped the snow from his boots,
took a pee and lit a smoke,
threw down the match and drove off
thinking that nobody
would ever know the difference.

december 8

Twenty degrees at sunrise.

All feathered out in clouds,
the wind's a mockingbird this morning.
Out of its mouth,
the piercing whistle of a red-tailed hawk,
the caw of a crow.
No hawk or crow to be seen
from one downy gray side of the sky
to the other.

december 9

Clear, still and cold.

Fence post to fence post,
just out of reach,
a bank swallow led me
into the sunrise.

Black, white and gray
like a half-burned love letter
floating up out of a fire,
she led me along.

I would like to have read
what was left of that message,
red on its feathery edges
with dawn.

december 12

Sunny, still and cold.

Found, on the gravel road I walked this morning,
one beer can, part full of frozen tobacco juice
that when I shook it came apart like chunks of amber,
and a quarter-sized piece from a fluted china plate,
with a soft pink rose the size of a pencil eraser
and a curl of flying, pale blue ribbon. In a nearby tree,
five noisy crows who had seen me stooping there
were busy creating a plausible story.

december 13

Clear and at the freezing point.

Just as a dancer, turning and turning,
may fill the dusty light with the soft swirl
of her flying skirts, our weeping willow----
now old and broken, creaking in the breeze----
turns slowly, slowly in the winter sun,
sweeping the rusty roof of the barn
with the pale blue lacework of her shadow.

december 14

Home from my walk, shoes off, at peace.

The weight of my old dog, Hattie----thirty-five pounds
of knocking bones, sighs, tremors and dreams----
just isn't enough to hold a patch of sun in its place,
at least for very long. While she shakes in her sleep,
it slips from beneath her and inches away,
taking the morning with it----the music from the radio,
the tea from my cup, the drowsy yellow hours----
picking up dust and dog hair as it goes.

december 15

Clear and thirty-four at 6 a.m.

An old moon, lying akilter
among a few pale stars,
and so quiet on the road
I can hear every bone in my body
hefting some part of me
over its shoulder. Behind me,
my shadow stifles a cough
as it tries to keep up,
for I have set out fast and hard
against this silence,
filling my lungs with hope
on this, my granddaughter's
birthday, her first, and the day
of my quarterly cancer tests.

december 17

Clear and twenty-four at sunrise.

A cold wind out of the west all night.
Where our row of Norwegian pines
lines the road, there were lots of joined pairs
of needles this morning, blown over the grass
and onto the shoulder, every pair
an elongated V, coated with frost,
and each pointing east southeast,
where, sure enough, the sun was rising.

december 18

Gusty and forty at dawn.

Sunlight like honey this morning,
and a stiff wind spreading it smoothly
over the bluestem. Two miles down wind
from Hartmann's quarry, I hear the exuberant
backing-up song of a dump truck,
and directly above me, a red-tailed hawk
responds with its lispy whistle.
Burnt red seed-heads of buckbrush,
green duckweed over the beaver pond,
Todd Halle's red combine parked on a hilltop
as if to show the sun the way----
the eye contains the world, in a space
no bigger than a baby's fist.

december 19

Cold, and snow in the air.

The cedars in the roadside ditches
are nearly black against the many grays
of this winter morning, but unlike
most things with darkness at their centers
they don't turn an impenetrable shell
to the light. Rather, like ink on wet paper,
their dark limbs bleed into the light,
reaching farther and farther
into the whiteness of lightly falling snow.

december 20

Ten degrees at sunrise, light snow flying.

The beaver's mound of brush and cornstalks
stands at the edge of silence this morning,
a pyramid on an untracked desert of snow
with black, open water shining beyond it.
Somewhere inside are the hidden mysteries:
an old yellow-toothed pharoah, wrapped up
in bandages of sleep, and on his shallow breath,
oily odor of tanbark and the priceless perfume
of summer willow leaves.

december 21

Clear and five degrees.

Perfectly still this solstice morning,
in bone-cracking cold. Nothing moving,
or so one might think, but as I walk the road,
the wind held in the heart of every tree
flows to the end of each twig and forms a bud.

december 22

Five below zero.

The cold finds its way through the wall
by riding nails, common ten-penny nails
through a wall so packed with insulation
it wouldn't admit a single quarter-note
from the wind's soprano solo. Yet you can touch
this solid wall and feel the icy spots
where the nails have carried the outside
almost into the house, nickel-sized spots
like the frosty tips of fingers, groping,
and you can imagine the face
of the cold, all wreathed in flying hair,
its long fingers spread, its thin blue lips
pressed into the indifferent ear
of the siding, whispering something
not one of us inside can hear.

december 23

Cold.

As if to spare the birds at the feeder
any more competition than they already have,
a snowflake drops right past the perches
crowded with finches, nuthatches, sparrows,
and without even thinking to open its wings
settles quietly onto the ground.

december 24

Well below freezing and still.

All night I heard tapping,
like a teacher at a blackboard:
a bad bearing, I guessed,
in the furnace fan.
But early this morning,
passing the kitchen window,
I discovered the fancy
football plays of frost
chalked onto the cold black glass.

december 25

Sunny and clear.

Sometimes, when things are going well,
the daredevil squirrel of worry
suddenly leaps from the back of my head
to the feeder, swings by his paws
and clambers up, twitching his question mark tail.
And though I try the recommended baffles----
tin cone of meditation, greased pipe
of positive thought----every sunflower seed
in this life is his if he wants it.

december 26

Clear and cold.

A little snap at one side of the room,
and an answering snap at the other:
Stiff from the cold and idleness, the old house
is cracking its knuckles. Then the great yawn
of the furnace. Even the lampshade is drowsy,
its belly full of a warm yellow light.

Out under the moon, though, there is at least
one wish against this winter sleep: A road
leads into the new year, deliberate as a bride
in her sparkling white dress of new snow.

december 27

Twenty degrees.

For the past two years there's been
a white chenille bedspread
caught up in a barbed wire fence
along the road to the quarry.
For a while it looked like a man
who had fallen asleep on a sofa,
sad bachelor uncle of a man,
the soft ball of his bald head fallen,
long thin arms stretched out
along the back and trembling.
But today that was gone, torn away
by the wind, and there was no one
but me on the road. My heart
flapped like a rag in my ears.

december 28

Windy and at the freezing point.

There are days when the world
has a hard time keeping its clouds on,
and its grass in place, and this
is one of them, tumbleweeds
huddled up under the skirts
of the cedars, oak trees
joining hands in the windy grove.
Even the dawn light, blocky
with pink and yellow and blue
like a comics section, quickly
fluttered away, leaving a Sunday
the color of news.

december 29

Windy and cold.

All night, in gusty winds,
the house has cupped its hands around
the steady candle of our marriage,
the two of us braided together in sleep,
and burning, yes, but slowly,
giving off just enough light so that one of us,
awakening frightened in darkness,
can see.

december 30

Two degrees and clear.

A box of holiday pears came yesterday,
twenty tough little pears, all red and green,
neatly nested in cardboard cubicles,
their stems all pointed the same direction
like soldiers, a shine on their faces.
Five, all in a row, had been singled out
for special commendation and were wrapped
in crumpled tissue parachutes. Maybe
these were the leaders, the first to leap
from the trees, singing their battle song,
Early this morning I lifted the lid
and they were sleeping peacefully, lying
on one hard side or the other, dreaming
their leafy, breezy dreams of home.

december 31

Cold and snowing.

The opening pages forgotten,
then the sadness of my mother's death
in the cold, wet chapters of spring.

For me, featureless text of summer
burning with illness, a long convalescence,
then a conclusion in which
the first hard frosts are lovingly described.

A bibliography of falling leaves,
an index of bare trees,
and finally, a crow flying like a signature
over the soft white endpapers of the year.

january

january 3

Two below zero at 5 a.m.

All through the night,
the deeply troubled, sighing furnace
has tried to console one whimpering floorboard
that wants to return to its tree.

Beyond the walls, milky, translucent snow,
brushed into drifts
by the long blue fingers of shadow.

The snow has gathered as much of the light as it can
from the stars, but that's not enough warmth
to kindle the eyes of even one rabbit,
frozen still as a stone at the corner of morning.

january 4

Four below zero.

My wife took an apple to work
this morning, hurriedly picking it
up and out of a plastic bag
on the kitchen counter, and though
she has been gone an hour,
the open bag still holds in a swirl
the graceful turn of her wrist,
a fountain lifting. And now I can see
that the air by the closet door
keeps the bell-like hollow she made
spinning into her winter coat
while pushing her apple through a sleeve
and back out into the ordinary.

january 5

Eighteen degrees at sunrise.

Hung from the old loading chute
is a lasso of rusty wire,
and caught in the grain of its boards
is a wisp of red hair, and the heavy,
dead knocking of hooves.

january 7

Five degrees and light snow.

An elaborate braiding of deer tracks
close to the house this morning early,
within a few yards of our two dogs
asleep on the porch. A dozen or more
walking soundlessly east in the night,
a half moon rising before them.
I like the long deft brush stroke
as each hoof swung into and out of the snow,
and the little splash kicked out ahead
as they stripped sweet bark from the darkness,
afraid of everything but not afraid.

january 8

Overcast and cold. New snow in the night.

A sudden gust, and a mulberry branch
shakes loose a length of snow
that somehow keeps the shape of the branch
as it falls, and soon another falls and then
another, a blue and white nuthatch
diving and dodging among them
as it flies to our feeder and back. And all of this
without a sound.

january 9

Clear and still.

Ten below zero at dawn, and the sky
like the skin of a pearl,
nobody warming the pearl in his hand
but leaving it spin on the black glass table
with all of us inside,
right down to me here at my window,
warming my hands on a cup,
right down to a goldfinch, green and gray,
no bigger than a breath,
picking a single thistle seed from the feeder,
right down to a thistle seed.

january 10

Eight degrees at 6 a.m.

Cloudy and cold, the moon like a lamp
behind a curtained window,
and who could be sitting alone in that room
with its dusty, ancient furniture
if not a god?

january 12

Thirty-two degrees at sunrise.

You can catch an owl
that's been killing your chickens
by setting a trap on a post
in your poultry yard
and that's all I can call up
to describe that funeral tent
alive and wildly struggling
in a punishing wind
just thirty-seven years ago
this morning, and we mourners
huddled in the shadow
of those wings.

january 13

One degree at 8 a.m.

All night these trees in the woodlot
have been the veins and arteries
of darkness, carrying darkness
out to the capillary twigs and into
the thick black leaves that filled the night
but that at dawn are falling,
blowing like shadows over the snow.

january 16

The January thaw.

A flock of several hundred small brown birds,
all of one mind, crazily chases its tail
across a muddy field and into a grove of trees.
They are full of joy, like a wheel that breaks loose
from a truck and bounds down the road
ahead of the driver, then eventually slows
and falls behind, wobbling onto a spot
on the shoulder, rocking around on its rim,
then settling with a ringing cry.

january 17

Dark and still at 5:30 a.m.

Some mornings, very early, I put on
my dead father's brown corduroy robe,
more than twenty years old, its lining torn,
the sleeves a little too long for me,
and walk through the house
with my father, groping our way
through the chilly, darkened rooms,
not wanting to waken our wives with a light,
and feeling on our outstretched fingers,
despite the familiar order of each room,
despite the warmth of women sleeping near,
the breath of emptiness.

january 18

Gusty and warmer.

Most of our snow will be gone by noon,
leaving its customary cast-offs: over there,
a white slab like the lid of a freezer;
here and there, newspapers soggy with rain.
In the shade of an empty farmhouse,
what looks to be a bedsheet, fresh with blueing,
and next to the road, a pair of very dirty panties.

january 19

Still thawing, breezy

Arthritic and weak, my old dog Hattie
stumbles behind me over the snow.
When I stop, she stops, tipped to one side
like a folding table with one of the legs
not snapped in place. Head bowed, one ear
turned down to the earth as if she
could hear it turning, she is losing the trail
at the end of her fourteenth year.
Now she must follow. Once she could catch
a season running and shake it by the neck
till the leaves fell off, but now they get away,
flashing their tails as they bound off
over the hill. Maybe she doesn't see them
out of those clouded, wet brown eyes,
maybe she no longer cares. I thought
for a while last summer that I might die
before my dogs, but it seems I was wrong.
She wobbles a little way ahead of me now,
barking her sharp small bark,
then stops and trembles, excited, on point
at the spot that leads out of the world.

january 21

Cloudy and still.

On the sunny, southerly face
of a cutbank, a badger
has scooped a new burrow,
turning the slope inside out
and pouring it full
of the very worst kind of darkness,
the kind the animals own,
like the mad black slit in a goat's eye.

january 23

Twenty-two degrees and very still.

The road like a levee this morning
two hours before dawn. In the distance,
whole farms float away on waves
of blue snow, their yardlamps sparkling
like starlight on water. Up close,
the wreck of an old barn lists to one side,
caught up in a tangle of trees,
and near it, a sheet of corrugated roofing
with its corners bent up at bow and stern,
begins its long voyage, bearing
the huddled figure of an engine block.

january 24

A pale half moon far in the west.

In this roadside churchyard,
the faint rumble of underground trains,
long trains of coffins linked like Pullman cars,
their windowshades drawn down,
slowly rolling under the grand, dripping arches
of cedar roots, then picking up speed
as they disappear into the clattering darkness.

january 25

Nineteen degrees at sunrise.

A rag rug of a landscape this morning----
remnants of dirty snow,
torn strips of muddy stubble field.
Behind the yellow windowshade of dawn,
in an enormous, sunny room,
my grandfather's older brother, Lou,
wearing a woman's apron, blue and white,
bends stiffly away from the loom
upon which he's weaving the day
and rummages through his bag of scraps.
He needs one with a spot of green
to show me down here on the gravel road
stepping along in my winter coat.

january 26

Overcast, cold and still.

A hundred yards ahead,
a coyote crosses the road at a lope,
stops on a rise, looks back,
runs on. It is less like
the shape of an animal running
than the shadow of something flying.
When I get to the place where I saw it,
no tracks in the snow.

january 27

Thirty-four degrees and clear.

Fifty or sixty small gray birds with crests
in a bare hackberry tree this morning early,
not one of them making a sound
or even the neat black silhouette of a sound
against the rising sun. They let me
walk up close, then one by one
they leapt from their perches and dropped
and caught the air and swung away
into the north, becoming a ribbon first,
and then, in the distance, confetti,
as they sprinkled their breathtaking silence
into another bare tree.

january 28

Twenty-eight degrees and breezy.

Looks like the wind pushed its way
right through this fence
and walked on down to the water.
On a barb there's a little scrap of hide
like a piece of cornshuck,
and at the edge of the pond,
the ice is open where its hooves broke through.

january 29

The blue moon. Windy.

In a rutted black field by the road,
maybe a dozen bulldozed hedge trees
have been stacked for burning----
some farmer wanting a little more room
for his crops----but the trees
are resisting, arching their spines
and flexing their springy branches
against settling so easily
into their ashes, into the earth,
so that there is a good deal more wind
in the pile than wood, more tree
than fallen tree, and the sparrows
fly in and out, still singing.

january 30

Twenty-five degrees.

This morning the world is made of wind,
nearly everything creaking or flying,
even the shingles vainly lifting
as if the house, which at dawn has bobbed
white-bellied to the wave-tossed surface,
were drawing wind into its gills.

january 31

Light mist on a sharp wind.

Where two fences meet at a corner,
two thickets of bare plum bushes
also have met, and have blended
to soften the corner with clouds
of wine red canes and purple thorns.
Two weeks ago, they pulled a snowstorm
down out of the wind and spread
a long soft drift beneath their branches,
and though by this morning the snow
had melted away from the field,
the drift sleeps, long and white and cold,
rounding the corner, an L shape
that gracefully tapers out to its ends
like a boomerang, a new one that never
flew back to the hand of the wind.

february

february 1

Breezy and cold.

New snow has draped its bed sheets
over a month's old furniture
and with its icy dead-bolt locked the house
where January lived.

february 4

Clear and windy.

I saw a dust devil this morning,
doing a dance with veils of cornshucks
in front of an empty farmhouse,
a magical thing, and I remembered
walking the beans in hot midsummer,
how we'd see one swirling toward us
over the field, a spiral of flying leaves
forty or fifty feet high, clear as a glass
of cold water just out of reach,
and we'd drop our hoes and run to catch it,
shouting and laughing, hurdling the beans,
and if one of us was fast enough,
and lucky, he'd run along inside the funnel,
where the air was strangely cool and still,
the soul and center of the thing,
the genie who swirls out of the bottle,
eager to grant one wish to each of us.
I had a hundred thousand wishes then.

february 5

Clear and windy.

In this graveyard, one old cedar,
its thick trunk looking as if
it were wrapped in narrow strips
of bleached out leather, pieces
of harness, perhaps, reins
tied there, layer upon layer
for more than a hundred years,
each horse nuzzling the same long grass
in the bright ringing of shovels.

february 6

Cloudy and still.

A light frost this morning,
and the pastures that awful February gray
that goes to the heart,
the gray of single mattresses
and the hair of forgotten old men.

february 7

Cloudy. Light rain in the night.

A noisy flock of starlings flies ahead
and then settles again.
They are especially wary this morning,
because they are moving
an entire 19th century garment factory
into the future,
carrying it from tree to tree,
complete with its hundreds of pairs
of scissors snipping,
the unceasing chitter of treadles,
and the whispers of girls.
The little panes of the high windows
glitter between the bare branches.

february 8

Clear and pleasant.

The reason the rooster is crowing
so desperately this morning,
his voice like a gate left open in the wind,
is because the rising sun
is displaying its colorful plumage,
spreading its wings for a thousand miles
along the horizon
and the eyes of every hen are lit with fire.

february 9

Clear, cold and still.

So still this morning that the wheel
of my neighbor's windmill
hums just a little but will not start
to turn, and all I can see
as I walk the next two miles
is my mother's old sewing machine

with its hum and its shining nickel wheel
that she would touch so absentmindedly
before it could begin to sew.

february 10

Cloudy, cool and very still.

Sometimes at night, my old dog Hattie
will lift her head to bark at nothing,
as if that nothing were silently
crossing the yard in the darkness,
and then she'll listen hard and bark again
until it steals away. This morning
I woke at three o'clock, and nothing
was standing there, silently watching me,
holding its breath at the foot of the bed.
I must have made some little noise
because my wife turned toward me and asked,
"What's wrong?" "Nothing," I answered,
and suddenly nothing was gone
and from below us Hattie barked and barked.

february 11

Windy and cold, with snow predicted.

Our finch feeder, full of thistle seed
oily and black as ammunition,
swings wildly in the wind, and the finches
in olive drab like little commandos
cling to the perches, six birds at a time,
ignoring the difficult ride.

february 12

Still windy, but clear.

Our big dog, Buddy, mostly white
but speckled and spotted brown
like a snowdrift dirty with road dust,
sleeps at my feet on a patterned carpet
a dozen shades of red and orange
as if it were woven of fallen maple leaves
or the flames from a fire of those leaves.
Is this smoke in my eyes?
What season of my life is this?

february 13

Breezy and pleasant.

At first light, the bare trees sway,
but not together.
Shifting their weight from side to side,
they are like a crowd
that has waited all night for a gate to open.

february 14

Sunny, but cool.

Under the feeder, the juncos
have scribbled all over the snow
while seeds spilled from above
like inspiration. This is the way
each delectable metaphor
so suddenly appears
right under the beak of the poet,
who flutters his tail with delight.

february 16

An early morning fog.

In fair weather, the shy past keeps its distance.
Old loves, old regrets, old humiliations
look on from afar. They stand back under the trees.
No one would think to look for them there.

But in fog they come closer. You can feel them
there by the road as you slowly walk past.
Still as fence posts they wait, dark and reproachful,
each stepping forward in turn.

february 18

Quiet and clear.

Dawn, and the snip-snip-snip of a chickadee
cutting a circle of light to line her nest.

february 19

Thirty-five degrees and drizzling.

When I switched on a light in the barn loft
late last night, I frightened four flickers
hanging inside, peering out through their holes.
Confused by the light, they began to fly
wildly from one end to the other,
their yellow wings slapping the tin sheets
of the roof, striking the walls, scrabbling
and falling. I cut the light
and stumbled down and out the door and stood
in the silent dominion of starlight
till all five of our hearts settled down.

february 21

Sunny and clear.

Fate, here I stand, hat in hand,
in my fifty-ninth year,
a man of able body and a merry spirit.
I'll take whatever work you have.

february 23

Six inches of new snow.

Some bird with feet the approximate gauge
of an H. O. train has laid a wavy track
along the side of the house, tooting the while,
or so I'd guess, and at the front porch door
a mouse has left its busy back-and-forth
and then dithered away. Crossing the yard,
a rabbit has hopped from one side of its course
to the other and back, as rabbits will,
avoiding the land mines. And each of our dogs,
always the ones for a touch of sentiment,
stepped out at dawn to leave a yellow peony.

february 24

Twenty-seven degrees and clear.

In the yard of the empty Walker place
the storm cellar roof has fallen in,
and the cut stone steps that once led down
to safety now lead to a wall of sod
and rubble. But in memory, the safe places
never fall into themselves. They remain
warmly lit by a lantern. Burlap bags
always full of potatoes, damp wooden shelves
jewelled with jars of preserves.

february 25

Sunny. The snow melting back.

The long, slanting light of midwinter
shines back at itself
from the tinned-over door of an old barn
among dead trees.

How many millions of miles has it travelled
only to find this dented mirror,

and then to have to pay these cottonwoods in silver.

february 26

Thirty-eight degrees at sunrise.

As if he were turning a key in a lock,
the old magician turns his fist and opens it
and shakes out a pink silk scarf,
then snaps it in the air to our applause.
Just so, our ancient Christmas cactus,
two months late, has suddenly shaken
a half dozen blooms from the tips
of its fingers. It was a gift from my father
twenty years ago, and I had begun to worry
that he had given up reminding us,
but this morning he's back in his place
in front of the mirror of time
where he snaps a pink silk handkerchief
and folds it into his jacket pocket.

february 28

Sunny and pleasant.

This morning, hundreds of geese are flying
in talkative lines. Each flock has the honor
of carrying a length of blue satin ribbon
representing the life of some very old person,
and each goose has a firm hold on one year.
When they need to rest and eat, they spiral down
into wet fields of stubble and lay out
the ribbons, reflecting the sky. In their rooms,
old men and old women, who all morning
have felt a cold wind blowing in their faces,
begin to warm, as if the sun were shining.

march

march 1

Clear and thirty-two at sunrise.

So far from the road
that its red was lost in the trees
like a spark in smoke,
a cardinal surprised me.
Out of a brushy hollow
three notes flew,
trailing a little after-whistle:
pachoo, pachoo, pachoo,
like the sounds a boy makes
playing guns. How far
those notes have travelled by now
is anybody's guess. They had
the force of Spring behind them
and a flat trajectory.

march 2

Patchy clouds and windy.

All morning
our house has been flashing in and out of shade
like a signal, and far across the waves of grass
a neighbor's house has answered,
offering help. If I have to abandon this life,
they tell me they'll pull me across
in a leather harness
clipped to the telephone line.

march 3

Clear and cold.

Two years ago this week, in the muddy fields
along the Platte, the farmers gathered up
thousands of dead sandhill cranes
killed by a sudden spring blizzard
and doused them with gas, and burned them.
The black heaps sparked and smoldered
every few hundred yards along the river,
the live cranes calling from the sky, and below,
the smoke indecisive, standing on thin legs,
leaning one way and then another.

march 5

Very windy and cold.

A flock of robins bobs in the top
of a wind-tossed tree,
with every robin facing north
and the sky flying into their faces.
But this is not straightforwardness,
nor is it courage, nor an example
of purpose and direction
against insurmountable odds.
They perch like this
to keep their feathers smooth.

march 7

Overcast, breezy and cold.

This morning I watched a red-tailed hawk,
wings back, drop like the head of a hatchet
into the ditch. Whatever she caught
in the deep dry grass, rabbit or mouse,
had a moment to lie there before it could die
while the hawk stretched to full height,
fanned and then leisurely folded her wings,
tipped her head with a gleaming yellow eye
and for a minute watched it waiting.

march 8

Thirty degrees and heavy snow.

The only sound against this stillness:
A crow flaps through our Norway pines,
its wingtips brushing snowflakes from the needles.

march 9

Eighteen and clear

Our broken apple tree
has caught what little snow it could
in its basket of sticks
as if to say
by holding out these soft wet blossoms
it still can lift and carry.

march 10

Quiet and cold at 6 a.m.

At dawn, in the roadside churchyard,
the recent, polished headstones glance and flash
as if the newly dead were waving pink placards
protesting the loss of their influence.
But the soft old marbles, grainy from weather
and losing their names, have a steady glow,
like paper bags with candles lit inside,
lining a path, an invitation.

march 11

Sunny and milder.

The sky a pale yellow this morning,
like the skin of an onion,
and here at the center,
under layer upon layer of brooding
and ferment, a poet,
and cupped in his hands, the green shoot
of one word.

march 12

5:30 a.m., dark and cold.

Only a crust of moon is left
to offer the morning,
but that may be enough for now,
what with our frosty picnic table
so heavily laden with stars.

march 13

Overcast and still.

High in an elm, a red-bellied woodpecker
rattles a branch, rattling and resting,
rattling and resting, each flat dry burst
like a single extended sound. It's the creak
of the painted wainscot ceiling
of my grandparents' porch, under the strain
of the chains of the swing. Somehow
it has carried this far, four hundred miles
and more than fifty years, the sound
of my Uncle Elvy watching the highway
and swinging, the toes of his good shoes
just touching the floor.

march 16

Snow melting from the roof.

Spring, the sky rippled with geese,
but the green comes on slowly,
timed to the ticking of downspouts.
The pond, still numb from months
of ice, reflects just one enthusiast
this morning, a budding maple
whose every twig is strung with beads
of carved cinnabar, bittersweet red.

march 18

Gusty and warm.

I saw the season's first bluebird
this morning, one month ahead
of its scheduled arrival. Lucky I am
to go off to my cancer appointment
having been given a bluebird, and,
for a lifetime, having been given
this world.

march 20

The vernal equinox.

How important it must be
to someone
that I am alive, and walking,
and that I have written
these poems.
This morning the sun stood
right at the end of the road
and waited for me.